Amazon Echo

ADVANCED USER GUIDE

*Step-by-Step Instructions
to Enrich your Smart Life*

By
Steve Wright

Table of Contents

WHY YOU NEED THIS BOOK

"Alexa, Wake me up at 6 am"

You wake up in the morning at 6 am with the sound of birds chirping. You get up and head straight to your kitchen where a freshly brewed cup of your favourite double espresso is waiting for you. While sipping coffee, Echo reads out the latest news flash and weather report. There is a forecast for rains so you decide to head over to your treadmill instead of going out for a run. In the mean time, your soft boiled eggs are ready and you have your breakfast while Echo reads out your calendar for the day. Next, you take a quick shower and then ask Echo to order a cab. The cab arrives and you head straight to office.

This is an average morning routine of a regular person, what makes this particular anecdote exceptional is that this was choreographed by Echo without the touch of a button.

Welcome to your SMART LIFE!

Amazon Echo is a voice-activated smart speaker. It is compatible with an ever increasing number of smart devices and online platforms. It can answer basic queries, control smart devices, stream music from any of your cloud accounts, and much more. It responds to the wake word "Alexa".

Alexa is a cloud-based, voice-activated personal assistant. Unlike Siri or other digital assistants, she has an incredible variety of skills and can be pre-programmed to carry out errands. As you start to use Echo, Alexa adapts to your speech patterns, vocabulary, and personal preferences. And you can also download and install third party Alexa Skills on your Echo device to enhance its capabilities!

This book is written for those who are puzzled by the Echo. First, are you one who wonders about automation or one who gets things done? Yes, the time for disposing off wires and switches has come. You enter the world of Echo, and Alexa, the wonderful assistant who switches off the lights out when you go to sleep and sends you a message when she senses smoke in the house. Are you ready to be amazed how easier Echo will make your life? Read on and find why the world is going one step smarter with the Amazon Echo.

Alexa combines with countless smart devices and apps to help you automate your daily life. So, let's begin the journey to discover how to use your Echo and Tap to its best advantage.

This book is written from my personal experience and anecdotal evidence from hundreds of fellow Echo Users who have helped me adapt this smart device into my life. Through this book, my goal is to help you setup Echo and start using it like a pro.

After reading this book you will be able to

- Connect all your smart devices at home and use Echo as your hub to control them.
- Pre-program regular errands like making coffee, reading your calendar and switching off lights at night.
- Shop on Amazon, order pizza and have fun with Easter Eggs.

Learn more, turn up the thermostat, open the shades and put on your favorite music...hmm "Alexa, turn the thermostat up..."

Chapter 1

GETTING STARTED WITH ECHO

Echo is a voice-activated speaker from Amazon that

- Acts as your smart personal assistant
- Performs digital errands at your command
- Connects and controls all of your smart devices

It brings a new dimension of supplementary ease to a smart home. Users can control settings of interconnected devices through a simple voice command. By doing away with dials, switches, and buttons, Echo helps multiple users with different accents activate or change settings on digital devices from far away.

For those who already have the Echo, here is an update. Most voice controlled devices used in computers, mobile phones, and cars will recognize as many as 50 commands. You can 'command' it with voice messages that last for 2 minutes at a time. You would know by now how amazing it feels to have an assistant that does exactly as told and it gets smarter with every interaction.

When things get this easy, most people ignore it. Yet, what stops you from taking the next step to the futuristic world? Echo has removed your wires, done away with switches, and opened a world of comfort at the touch of a button...and even easier by issuing a command!

- With music playing, or in the midst of a conversation, Echo hears, recognizes and obeys your voice
- Play music, 360° immersive-audio-sound that is Omni-directional
- Control just about anything – Samsung SmartThings, thermostat having compatible WeMo
- Use Echo to switch lights and electrical devices on or off
- Work with Insteon, Nest, Wink, Ecobee and Philips Hue smart devices
- Voice control for hands-free operation
- Get answers to questions and catch the news
- Read audiobooks out and catch up with the latest sports news through Alexa Voice Service
- Constant upgrade of service features and skills with the latest as Domino's and Uber

Echo Basics

The cost of the Amazon Echo is $179.99. Amazon has also introduced a portable version called Amazon Tap, which can be carried around. You can either use an intelligent battery base or a 21W power adapter for your Echo unit. The intelligent battery base powers your Echo for 6 hours and costs $49.99 – $54.99 on Amazon. The adapter is $19.99. Pay $29.99 for the voice remote for Echo (also works with Echo Dot).

Echo, a hands-free operative speaker-microphone device, is a 9.25-inch cylindrical metal container that is 3.27 inches in diameter. Since it stands upright on its circular face, it takes up as much space as the bottle containing your vitamin tablets. It weighs a little over a kilogram (1064g or 37.5 oz.). Use the 6-feet long power cable to get going.

Bluetooth and Wi-Fi connections

Echo works with Fire OS or any iOS devices. In addition, you may use Android systems or your computer browser to connect. Echo has both Wifi and Bluetooth connectivity. The MIMO Wi-Fi dual antennae drop fewer connections compared to standard Wi-Fi connections. Supported Wi-Fi networks are 802.11 a/b/g/n.

Since it does not support peer-to-peer connections, you cannot use voice commands to connect and convey orders to another device through your Echo.

Bluetooth connectivity Amazon Echo and Audio/Video Remote Control Profile (AVRCP) receives audio streaming from your mobile device to control connected audio devices through voice control.

However, Mac OS X devices cannot be used for voice control. Use the Advanced Audio Distribution Profile (A2DP) to begin voice streaming.

Setup your Echo

1. Plug in Echo

Connect the power cord to the bottom and place it in a central location. Try to find a place at least 10 inches from the walls, windows or any obstructions. Once the location is finalised, plug in the Echo. The LED light ring on top of your Echo will turn blue and then orange. Once it turns orange, Echo will greet you.

Buttons on Echo

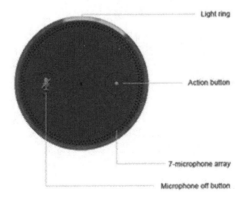

You will have two buttons on top of the cylinder. One is the action button while the other is the microphone button.

By depressing the microphone button once, Echo will be on MUTE and the light will turn red. Press once more to turn the microphone on. You use the action button to do activities such as:

- Wake your device
- Turn on or off an alarm

- Set up Wi-Fi mode by pressing and holding the button for 5 seconds

At the base of the cylinder, just above your wire connecting to the power socket, you have a LED bulb. This will be white when connected to the Wi-Fi. If not, the color will be orange. When it has Wi-Fi connection but cannot access Alexa, this light will blink in orange color.

Downloading the Alexa App

Now, go to the store on your mobile or computer. This could be Google Play Store, Apple App Store or Amazon Appstore. Instead, you can type**alexa.amazon.com** in your browser search bar. Search and download the *Alexa app* for Fire OS, Android or iOS. Sign into your account and follow the instructions in the app/website to complete the setup.

(Please note that Alexa app is not supported on Kindle Fire 1st or 2nd Generations)

Setting Up Echo

2. Connect to the internet
with the Alexa App

Be sure to connect dual-band Wi-Fi networks and not use mobile hotspots. It will not work when you use ad-hoc networks that are connected peer-to-peer.

- Open the Alexa app and go to **Settings**.
- Select your device and click on **Update Wi-Fi**.
- For first time users, click on **Select a new device**.
- Now, press the *Action* button on the Echo device.
- The light will turn orange and you will see a list of networks appear on your mobile device. Select your Wi-Fi network and type the password if required.
- For cases where your network is not visible, scroll down the list and select **Add a Network**.
- If this does not work, click on **Rescan**.
- Now click **Connect** and Alexa is ready for use.

Decoding the LED Light Ring

Different colours on the LED ring tell you what your Amazon Echo is doing.

- Echo is **Starting Up**: Revolving cyan light on a blue background.
- Echo is processing your request and is **busy**: Cyan light with a blue background in the direction of the person speaking.
- Echo connecting to **WiFi**: Clockwise Revolving orange light
- Echo on **MUTE**: Red light
- Echo adjusting volume: White Light
- Echo is detecting error while setting up the WiFi: Oscillating purple light.
- Echo awaiting your request: No Light.

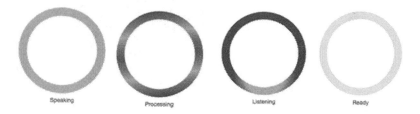

Volume Ring

- Turn clockwise to increase volume
- Turn anticlockwise to reduce volume

Connect to Bluetooth

You can pair your mobile device (smart phone or tablet) with Amazon Echo. Turn on the Bluetooth for your mobile device and ensure your mobile device is in range. Use the following commands.

- "Alexa, pair Bluetooth"
- "Alexa, disconnect my phone / tablet"
- "Alexa, connect my phone / tablet"

Checking Alexa

Go to **echosim.io**. Here you will see the Alexa symbol. Click on the symbol and give any voice command. If your Echo is working, then you will see the response.

Talk to Your Echo for the First Time

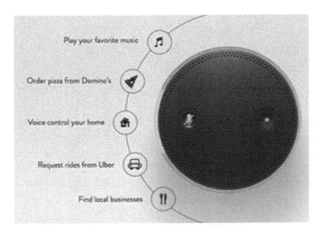

To begin, we use the wake word – *Alexa*. *'Alexa, play me some music'*. Or *'Alexa, what is the weather like today?'* When your voice reaches Echo, the circular, blue LED lights on top of Echo lights up – she is listening, and once your command is analysed, Alexa will reply.

Alexa listens every second for her 'wake' word through her seven microphones. This way you do not have to raise your voice and can call her over the din of conversation or music. If many people ask her questions, Alexa picks out the individual accents of the people and separates the questions with ease. Then, you get the answers. *"Music playing"* and *"The weather is sunny with day temperatures of 90 degrees."*

How to Change the Wake Word

To achieve this change on your mobile or computer

- Open Alexa app.
- Go to the control panel.

- On the left, you will see a list.
- Select **Settings** for the Echo device for which you want to change the 'wake word'.
- You will see Wake Word listed for each device.
- Click on this and select the new 'wake word'.
- Now click **Save.**
- This change is possible only on Echo and Dot.

Working with the remote

The remote has a microphone, a talk button, and Playback controls. To talk, you press the talk button and talk. The playback button helps you to Play or Pause, Increase or Decrease the Volume, and switch to Next or Previous. The advantage when you use the remote is that you need not 'wake' up Alexa with the 'wake word'. Now, by default the 'wake word' is 'Alexa' but you can change it to 'Amazon' or 'Echo'. This proves invaluable for those who have more than one Echo units and do not want to disturb the one on the top floor when 'talking' the one in your living room.

How to Setup Voice Purchasing

You can buy digital and physical products from Amazon with your Alexa device using the 1-click payment method. You need a US billing address and a payment method and Prime Membership (only for Physical Products) to enable voice transactions.

When you register your Alexa device, Voice Purchasing is on by default.

You can use voice commands to carry out the following activities with your Echo

- **Purchase** a Prime-eligible Item
- **Reorder** an Item
- **Add** an Item to your Amazon cart
- **Track** the Status of a Recently Shipped Item
- **Cancel** an order immediately after ordering it.

To Enable/Disable Voice Purchasing, activate an optional 4-digit confirmation code and check your payment method and billing address

- Open the Alexa App
- Tap Settings
- Voice Purchasing

Now you can access all the purchase settings, to make any required changes.

A few Categories in the physical products are **NOT ELIGIBLE** for voice purchasing.

- Apparel
- Prime Pantry
- Shoes
- Watches
- Prime Now
- Jewellery
- Amazon Fresh
- Add-On items

Now that you are all set for Voice Purchasing!

These are few commands you can use to make your first purchase on Echo.

Shopping Commands

- *"Alexa, order (item name)"*
- *"Alexa, reorder (item name)"*
- *"Alexa, add (item name) to my cart"*
- *"Alexa, track my order "*
- *"Alexa, where is my stuff?"*
- *"Alexa, cancel my order"*

Manage your Shopping/To Do List

- Tap the main menu on your Echo App
- Select Shopping & To-do Lists

You can add, remove or edit items on the list in the App itself or by using the voice commands. You can export these listsusing IFTTT recipes on **ifttt.com** to:

- **Evernote**- *bit.ly/amzeco1*
- **Gmail**- *bit.ly/amzeco2*
- **Todoist**- *bit.ly/amzeco3*
- **ios Reminders**- *bit.ly/amzeco4*

Tap and Echo

Echo is not a portable device, although now you can find portable power source solutions for your Echo. Amazon Tap is the portable version of Echo to help you when you are on the move. This is smaller and has its own charging cradle and weighs about half of the Amazon Echo because of the size of the speakers.

The Echo has a 2.5-inch woofer and a 2-inch tweeter while the Tap has speakers that are 1.5 inches. While both connect to the local Wi-Fi network, the Tap goes one step further. It connects to mobile networks through the mobile hotspots. So, it keeps working even when Wi-Fi is not present. Then there is the name Tap, which implies you have to 'tap' the unit to connect with Alexa. In the Echo, Alexa is always listening. You don't have to tap it.

Alexa Commands

You can make these commands work on all Alexa enabled devices: Echo, Tap and Dot. Just use the following commands.

- *"Alexa, Stop"*
- *"Alexa, Volume [number Zero to Ten]"*

- *"Alexa, Unmute"*
- *"Alexa, Mute"*
- *"Alexa, Repeat"*
- *"Alexa, Cancel"*
- *"Alexa, Louder"*
- *"Alexa, Volume Up"*
- *"Alexa, Volume Down"*
- *"Alexa, Turn Down"*
- *"Alexa, Turn Up"*
- *"Alexa, Help"*

How to Get Help from Alexa

When you've got a question about your Echo, you can simply ask Alexa about it.

To get some help from Alexa, just say the ***Alexa***word followed by the following questions:

- *"What can you do?"*
- *"What are your new features?"*
- *"What do you know?"*
- *"Can you do math?"*
- *"How can/do I play music?"*
- *"How can/do I add music?"*
- *"What is Prime Music?"*
- *"What is Audible?"*
- *"What is Connected Home?"*
- *"What is Voice Cast?"*
- *"How can/do I pair to Bluetooth?"*
- *"How can/do I connect my calendar?"*
- *"What is an Alexa skill?"*
- *"How can/do I use skills?"*
- *"How can/do I set an alarm?"*

Alexa SKILL Commands

Your Amazon Echo comes with a set of built in abilities. To enhance these abilities or to add new abilities to your Echo add new Alexa Skills that are developed by Amazon or third party Skills developers. You can find these Skills on your Alexa App.

These skills are the Alexa equivalent of iOS/Android Apps for your Smart Phone. Alexa Skills development is still in its infancy but this platform is developing fast. As more and more people buy Echo and Amazon launches it in multiple countries, you will see a sudden surge in the number of skills for Alexa.

All skills support Launch command and Stop command and majority support the Help command.

Launch

Just say….

- "Alexa, launch [skill name]"

The skill will be launched and you will come to know that hearing the welcome message for the particular skill. Some information about the skill and applicable sample commands will be included in the message.

Stop

This one is straightforward. One quick hack: you can actually say *"Alexa, Stop"* even when Echo is speaking. Just be loud enough so that Alexa is able to hear you out over her voice.

Help

Most of the Alexa Skills have a help function except some Skills, which are pretty straightforward. To access this help, just say, "Help," and Alexa will read out the particular Skill's Help file to you.

How to Reset Your Echo

The reset button for Echo is located at the bottom where the A/C power cord plugs in. Use a paperclip to press on it for 5 seconds and your Echo will reset.

How to Ensure Alexa Stops Listening

Press the MUTE button on top of the Echo. The top LED ring will turn red when the mute is ON. You can unmute by pressing the same button again.

How to Enforce Updates of Software

The Alexa software is updated periodically on its own, but sometimes there can be a delay between the release of new updates and your device receiving them. In such a scenario you can force update by keeping the Echo on Mute for 30 minutes.

How to Ask Alexa for basic Calculations

- *"Alexa, one thousand eight hundred seventy six (1,876) divided by four"*
- *"Alexa, three point four eight six (3.486) times twenty four"*
- *"Alexa, convert 12 feet to centimetres"*
- *"Alexa, convert 7 tablespoons to millilitres"*
- *"Alexa, convert 35 Fahrenheit to Celsius"*
- *"Alexa, how many miles are in thirty kilometres?"*

How to Ask Alexa for Cooking Conversions

- *"Alexa, how many teaspoons in two tablespoon?"*
- *"Alexa, how many tablespoons in eighteen teaspoons?"*
- *"Alexa, how many pints in four gallons?"*
- *"Alexa, how many cups in four quarts?"*

How to Hear Flash Briefings

To hear flash briefings of the latest new updates, you can configure your Echo App to include news from various sources: BBC, Economist, TMZ, and NPR etc. To hear the news, just say "Alexa, what's my Flash Briefing?" and Echo will play the news from your selected sources.

Configuring Flash Briefings

- Open the Alexa app
- Tap the left navigation panel,
- Goto Settings
- Select **Flash Briefing**
- Customize your Flash Briefing: Shows, News Headlines, Weather Updates etc

How to Sports Scores

Echo can tell you the scores from live matches and schedules of your favourite teams. Just ask

- *"Alexa, what the score (team name) game?"*
- *"Alexa, when does (team name) play?"*

How to get Localized Information

This feature works only if you are based in USA.

- Goto Settings in the Echo App
- Tap on Echo Device Location
- Enter your Zip Code
- Tap Save Changes

This will get you weather reports, local news and even pre-recorded shows relative to your area.

How to Configure the Traffic Information

To get the most efficient routes from your Echo

- Goto settings on your Echo App

- Tap on Change Address
- Input the address in the FROM and TO fields
- Tap Save Changes

This will get you the most accurate traffic information for your desired route

How to Read Kindle Books

- "Alexa, Read my Kindle book"
- *"Alexa, Read my book <title>"*
- *"Alexa, Play the Kindle book <title>"*
- *"Alexa, Read < title>"*

How to Listen to your Audiobooks

- *"Alexa, Read <title>"*
- *"Alexa, Play the book <title>"*
- *"Alexa, Play the audiobook <title>"*
- *"Alexa, Play <title> from Audible"*

Chapter 2

SMART HOME WITH ECHO

People have discovered the ease of managing and using smart devices in their homes by allowing Echo to become the command centre of their smart lives. You can control your thermostat, hue lights, garage door and every Wi-Fi compatible device connected with your Echo.

Let look at a few example of what is possible with Alexa....

You can control your smart home from anywhere using your smartphone or tablet. This excitement begins with the morning coffee and sets your lights in the home.

- Unlock/Lock the door using**Smart Danalock Recipes** that give you control over your doors. You can auto-unlock your door or lock your door at a specific time. You can use Echo, Dot or Tap to control these features. To access these recipes go to *ifttt.com/danalock*.
- You can use **D-Link Smart Plugs** to connect to other smart devices such as Netatmo Thermostat, Weather, Netatmo Welcome, and OnHub. To access go to *ifttt.com/dlink_smart_plug*.
- **GE Appliances Refrigerator Channel**: This channel lets you do many things such as blink the light if fridge door is open for a long time or use Alexa to set the fridge to Sabbath mode. To access go to *ifttt.com/ge_appliances_refrigerator*.
- The **Weather Channel** can help you set the coffeemaker on at sunrise, turn on Smart Plug at sunset, and if temperature or humidity rises, switch on the air conditioning by itself. To access go to *ifttt.com/ weather*.
- The **Netatmo Welcome** helps you identify visitors to the house and changes its behaviour for each instance. For example, if this person arrives, switch Smart Plug off (or on), and if unknown person arrives to turn on D-Link Smart Plug. To access go to *ifttt.com/ netatmo_welcome*.
- Get a notification on your smartphone if there is motion within your house.

Before you can execute these Smart Home Hacks, you will need to connect a number of devices to Alexa and then use the Alexa Skills and IFTTT Recipes to control these devices in creative ways.

Connect Devices to Alexa

To build your Smart Home, choose the Smart Devices you want to control from Amazon Echo and connect them to your Alexa App directly or through a Smart Hub. Following is a list of devices you can choose from.

Devices Directly Controlled by Alexa

Following are the Smart Devices that can be directly controlled by Alexa via WiFi.

Lighting and Fans

- LIFX WiFi Smart LED Light Bulbs
- Haiku WiFi Ceiling Fans

Switches and Outlets

- Belkin WeMo: Light Switch, Switch (Smart Plug) and Insight Switch
- TP-Link: Smart Plug and Smart Plug with Energy Monitoring
- D-Link WiFi Smart Plugs

Thermostats

- Nest Learning Thermostat
- Ecobee3 Smarter WiFi Thermostat
- Sensi WiFi Programmable Thermostat

Locks

- Garageio
- Danalock

Car Control

- Automatic

How to Connect Smart Devices to Alexa

- Make an account for your Smart Device on its native app.
- Connect your Smart Device account to Amazon account.
- Use voice commands or the Alexa App to control the Smart Device.

Devices that need a Hub/Bridge to be Controlled by Alexa

Lightning

- Philips Hue Series via Philips Hue Bridge/Starter Kit
- Cree Connected LED via Samsung SmartThings Hub or Wink Hub
- GE Link Bulb via Wink Hub
- Osram Lightify Smart Bulb via Wink Hub
- TPC Connected Smart Bulbs via Samsung SmartThings Hub or Wink Hub

Outlets, Dimmers and Switches

- iHome Smart Plug via Wink Hub
- Samsung SmartThings Outlet via Samsung SmartThings Hub
- Insteon Switches, Dimmers and Outlets via Insteon Hub

- GE Z-Wave Switches, Dimmers and Outlets via Samsung SmartThings Hub
- Leviton Switches, Dimmers and Outlets via Samsung SmartThings Hub or Wink Hub

Thermostats

- Honeywell Lyric/Total Connect Comfort Thermostats via Samsung SmartThings Hub
- Keen Home Smart Vents via Samsung SmartThings Hub

Why You Need a Smart Home Hub?

Smart Hubs are necessary because a lot of Smart Devices in the market lack the radios required to enable direct communication with Alexa. Until we have devices that can directly communicate with your Alexa, these hubs serve the purpose.

Alexa can control lots of smart home devices, but most of the integrations require a smart home hub that acts as a link between Echo and the particular device.

Here is a list of prominent Smart Home Hubs you can buy today to and control your Smart Home Devices:

- Samsung SmartThings Hub
- Wink Hub

- Insteon Hub
- Philips Hue bridge/Starter Kit
- Caseta Wireless Smart Bridge
- Alarm.com Hub
- Vivint Hub
- Nexia Home Intelligence Bridge
- Universal Devices ISY Hubs
- HomeSeer Home Controllers
- Simple Control Simple Hub
- Almond Smart Home WiFi Routers

How to connect your Smart Home Hub with Alexa

For simplicity, we are only demonstrating how to connect the *"Samsung SmartThings Hub"* with your Alexa; any other hub will have a similar procedure.

In the Amazon Alexa app

- Tap the menu (three horizontal lines in the top left)
- Tap **Smart Home**
- Scroll to Your Smart Home Skills
- Tap **Get More Smart Home Skills**
- Enter "SmartThings" in the search field
- Tap **Enable for SmartThings**
- Enter your SmartThings email and password
- Tap Log in
- Choose your **SmartThings Location** from the menu
- Tap the checkbox for each device Amazon Alexa needs access to
- Tap **Authorize**
- Once authorized, the following message appears: *"Alexa has been successfully linked with SmartThings."*
- Tap X to close the window and begin device discovery

How to Discover Devices

Open the Amazon Alexa app:

- In the previous step, after closing the success message, the Alexa app automatically directs you to discover devices
- Tap Discover Devices
- Wait for device discovery to complete

If not automatically prompted:

- In the Amazon Alexa app, tap the menu
- Tap Smart Home
- Scroll to Your Devices
- Tap Discover devices
- Wait for device discovery to complete

When discovery is complete, the discovered devices will list under the Your Devices section of Smart Home.

Voice Commands to Control your Smart Devices

- *"Alexa, turn off/on the bedroom light"*
- *"Alexa, brighten/dim the kitchen light"*
- *"Alexa set the bedroom light to 12 (Brightness scale of 0 - 100.)"*
- *"Alexa, lower/raise kitchen thermostat by 15 degrees"*
- *"Alexa, set kitchen thermostat to 74 degrees"*

How to Add New Devices

After connecting your Alexa device, you can use the Samsung SmartThings app to change/update which SmartThings devices Alexa can control.

If you add a new dimmer switch, on/off switch or thermostat to your existing SmartThings setup, use these steps to give Alexa access to the new device.

In the SmartThings App

- Tap the menu

- Tap SmartApps
- Tap Amazon Echo
- You will see all the devices Alexa has access to
- Tap My Switches or My Thermostats
- Tap the checkbox for each device Alexa needs access to
- Tap Done
- Tap Next
- Say: "Alexa, discover new devices"
- Wait for Alexa to confirm discovery is complete
- Tap Done

Disconnect SmartThings from Amazon Alexa

Uninstalling Alexa from Samsung SmartThings app will remove the connection between Alexa and your smart devices: your smart devices will no longer respond to voice commands for SmartThings devices.

How To disconnect in the SmartThings app

- Tap the menu
- Tap SmartApps
- Tap Amazon Echo
- Tap Uninstall
- Tap Remove
- Confirm removal

How To disconnect in the Amazon Alexa app

- Tap the menu (three horizontal lines in the top left)
- Tap Smart Home
- Scroll to Your Smart Home Skills
- Tap Disable for SmartThings
- Tap Disable Skill to confirm

Control Your Devices

Basic Voice Commands

The following list of commands works really well with Alexa and have been tested.

ON Commands

- "Alexa, turn on <Device Name>"
- "Alexa, start <Device Name>"
- "Alexa, unlock <Device Name>"
- "Alexa, open <Device Name>"
- "Alexa, boot up <Device Name>"
- "Alexa, run <Device Name>"
- "Alexa, arm <Device Name>"

OFF Commands

- "Alexa, turn off <Device Name>"
- "Alexa, stop <Device Name> (this one is tricky to get right)"
- "Alexa, stop running <Device Name> (also very tricky)"
- "Alexa, lock <Device Name>"
- "Alexa, close <Device Name>"

- "Alexa, shutdown <Device Name>"
- "Alexa, shut <Device Name>"
- "Alexa, disarm <Device Name>"

DIM Commands

- "Alexa, brighten <Device Name> to <Position>"
- "Alexa, dim <Device Name> to <Position>"
- "Alexa, raise <Device Name> to <Position>"
- "Alexa, lower <Device Name> to <Position>"
- "Alexa, set <Device Name> to <Position>"
- "Alexa, turn up <Device Name> to <Position>"
- "Alexa, turn down <Device Name> to <Position>"

IFTTT commands Integration with Alexa

IFTTT interface provides the easiest way to link various apps and functions with Alexa.

There are plenty of IFTTT recipes that you can use with Echo to automate your life and carry out repeatable tasks to save time and effort. But first you need to connect your Amazon account with IFTTT.

- Goto IFTTT and setup an account if you don't have one
- Goto channels home page and select Amazon Alexa channel
- This will prompt you to enter your Amazon account info to sign in

- Once your sign in you can access all the existing recipes for Alexa
- Choose from among 800+ recipes and add them to your account

Temperature Control with Nest Thermometer

You choose a phrase and the temperature you want. Then, you say,

- "Alexa, set [phrase]"

And your room temperature is set according to your wish.

For doing this, first, go to the **ifttt.com** and connect to the respective Nest channel.

- Open the Amazon Alexa Channel with your smartphone or computer.
- To do this, click on the three horizontal lines on the top left corner.
- Scroll down and choose Smart Home option.
- You come to the Device Links tab.
- Under this select Nest and click Continue.
- Log in with the Nest id and password.
- Now, you see Discover Devices.
- If Nest is on the local Wi-Fi network, Alexa will discover it.

You set the phrase to change the temperature

- "Alexa, set room temperature to 74 degrees now"

Automate your Life with SIGNUL Beacon channel

It is an amazingly unique way of creating a bridge between your physical and digital world just by detecting the presence or absence of your smartphone.

Define your zone entry and exit events to Signul Beacon to help automate mundane tasks. The Channel will use your physical context to streamline your digital world.

Here are things you can do once this you fix up this channel.

- Upon reaching your desk, you are logged into a spread sheet
- Slack is informed when you arrived for work
- When you arrive home, turn on the lights
- At bedtime, mute phone
- When you leave work, turn on Nest thermostat

To execute these hacks, connect to **Signul Beacon Channel** (*ifttt.com/signul_beacon*)on your IFTTT account and start using it.

Group the Lights Together

After work in the attic, when you get ready for bed, you want to switch out the lights. Not only those on the top floor, but also those in the porch and the hallway. Group them together and switch them all out by one voice command.

Echo will work with any smart connected device linked to your home Wi-Fi network. But Amazon offers support only for a few lights and switches, the rest need to be controlled through a Smart Hub as mentioned earlier. These are BR30 downlights, Hue H19 traditional bulbs, Light and Bloom Strips, and Lux white bulbs. If you plan to use switches go with WeMo. The range includes LightSwitch, Insight Switch, and Switch.

Use Wink to group your lights and control your bulbs. You must connect it to Echo. You can use this with GE Link bulbs if you so desire. You can even do more things such as opening blinds other than just open and close doors or switch lights on and off with the Wink App. Name each of the bulbs and give this group one name.

To Group the Lights

- Open the Echo app and click on Settings.
- Here you must find Connected Home.
- Add Wink. It will find Connected Devices.
- Now, you can add your Group.

Once you do this, you can Alexa commands and they will be executed

- "Alexa, turn on hall lights"

In this way, you can schedule a program to turn off the lights or use a single voice command such as, "Alexa, turn off all the lights" just before you go to bed.

House lights go on at sunset

Set your lights to go off at sunrise and on at sunset by the use of WeMo switches. You can control one or a group of lights and since they do not require batteries as they are WiFi controlled, they can operate forever. You can use any brand of light, fluorescent, halogen, LED, incandescent, and fans with the WeMo switch. The program works well even if you experience a power outage. However, you cannot replace three-way switches.

Download the WeMo app from Google Play or iOS for your Smart phone. You can turn on WeMo or turn it off. But first, you have to connect the **Wink Relay Channel**(*ifttt.com/relay)* and the **WeMo Switch Channel**(*ifttt.com/wemo_switch*) on IFTTT. While we are here, you should know that Wink Relay channel fits well with WeMo switches, Android SMS, Tesco, Sensibo, Yo and EVE for Tesla. You can do many items of work by the mere push of a button.

Turn Hue Lamps Red or Green

Magic begins when you change the ambiance with just a single command. Alexa will turn your Philips Hue Lamp Green, Red or turn them off when you want. But, connect the **Philips Hue Channel**(*ifttt.com/*hue) and your IFTTT**Workflow Channel** (*ifttt.com/wemo_switch*) first.

How to Use Yonomi with Alexa

Alexa seems somewhat reluctant clubbing the Switch ON and Switch OFF routines. You must write the programs separate and hope that they work. But, by combining Yonomi with Alexa you get a lot more things done.

The way to do this is to create the routines first in Yonomi. Name this with the room name say, Hall. In this, you turn on the Sonos, the light bulbs, and the fan. After you have done this, you do the turn off routine where you stop Sonos and turn off the light bulb and fan. Name this as Hall Off. When you turn on Echo discovery, it will map both these events to one device. Now, you can use Echo to turn on the hall lights with "Alexa, turn on Hall" and then turn them off with "Alexa, turn off Hall." Simple!

Setting up Alexa through Yonomi

- Open the Yonomi app
- Tap on the icon present at the top left corner
- You must now select the Accounts and Hubs Tab.
- Tap at the bottom right-hand corner (upper right-hand corner if you use iOS).
- Now choose Amazon Echo Account.
- Give your password and access your account.
- Now click on Connect.

Now use Echo to tell "Alexa, discover my devices." There you are, all done.

Adding Devices

If you haven't done so already, here are devices you can add to your smart home. You will find all these under WeMo and devices in IFTTT

WeMo Devices

- Crockpot: You can add two different commands: one to cook slow and the other to turn it off. This helps you control your crockpot.
- Maker: With this you can turn on, turn off and let the appliance run for a while. You must set the appropriate

command as "Alexa, turn on (off) the sprinklers" or "Alexa, set pool pump for 20."

- Coffeemaker: This helps you brew coffee.
- Switch: Plug any device you wish to control into the WeMo Switch such as turn on a lamp in the morning at 7 AM or turn on lights when I arrive home.

Sonos

- "Alexa, play the front room Sonos"
- "Alexa, set my living room Sonos to 40"

Quirky Aros

- "Alexa, turn on Aros"
- "Alexa, turn off Aros"
- "Alexa, set Aros to 80"

Alexa Skills for Smart Home Control

Alexa Skills are like Apps for your Echo that you can use to carry out advanced controls from your Echo.

Grouping your devices

If you have a SmartHome, *Group* the devices first. Through the *Group* Alexa will control operations of your SmartHome. Connect the apps you already have. Each of these apps will have a set of commands. For instance, Alexa controls LIFX lights with commands such as, *"Alexa turn the lights on," "Alexa, dim bedroom lights by 25%,"* or *"Alexa, Turn Kitchen light off."* However, there are concerns that Alexa has problems controlling over one light at a time at the time of writing this.

Nest

You may find that Alexa does not discover your Nest apps unless you name them right when you start. Use the term 'set' and then 'thermostat' (rename your thermostat to 'thermostat' if you have another name for it) and then call out the command. *'Alexa, set the thermostat to 80 degrees,'* or *'Alexa, cool down the master bedroom'* and so on.

Harmony

This app lets you group and name activities in your home. You can combine thermostats, lights, television, movies, blinds, or music. After doing this you can use a variety of commands such as *"Alexa, Start Harmony Activity"* , *"Alexa, End Harmony Activity"*, and *"Alexa, Use location to start Harmony Activity"*.

SmartThings

Much similar to Harmony, the SmartThings app lets you control electronics, lights, and everyday events with your smartphone. You can unlock the door with #hashtag, turn on a light when WeMo detects motion, get a phone call when SmartThings detect moisture.

Integrate with Home Control Assistant

The Home Control Assistant (HCA) links well with Alexa. At present, it has many features that work without Alexa but it helps improve your SmartHome. These are features apart from voice control for Alexa such as control for iPad, Windows, Android and iPhone. HCA helps you run several instances that involve the state of your house, location, time and event into one program. To do this, go to alexa.amazon.com and click on **Enable Skill**.

EventSeeker

For people who like action, EventSeeker helps them narrow things down with the help of Alexa. Alexa will read out the events in the category of your choice and you can find out what is happening in your locality and when it occurs. You do not have to sweat to find out the events you would like to attend. It's as simple as eating pie.

Track your things

Use a mix of *TrackR Bravo Tags* and *TrackR Atlas Plugs* to find things like your purse, keychain, car keys or your pet cat. *TrackR Atlas Plugs* map the house. You place *TrackR Bravo Tags* on selected items. Once you do this, you can find these items by asking Alexa, *"Alexa, where are my car keys?"* and you get, *"Your car keys are on the living room sofa."* While the *Atlas Plugs* cost $39 per piece the *Tags* cost $29 each.

Chapter 3

GO TO WORK WITH ECHO

Named by Mashable as the best tech product 2015, Echo stands tall and for now alone in voice control.

How to Connect your Google Calendar to Alexa

Though you can use any calendar you like, the Google Calendar will help you take the first step.

To connect follow these simple steps:

- Open the Echo App in your mobile
- Click on *Settings>Calendar>Link GoogleCalendar Account*

You log in with your Google account and when you activate Alexa, you can check your schedule though you cannot write in new events. For that, you need to integrate the IFTTT recipe **Add Amazon Echo To-Do to Google Calendar**(*bit.ly/amzeco100*)

There are other recipes as well that can come handy, such as Add your ToDo list to Google Calendar or Add a Sports Game to your Google Calendar. To check the complete list please visit**ifttt.com**.

Do this on your calendar

"Alexa, what's on my calendar?" or *"Alexa, when is my next event?"* will give you the answers, *"You have a golf game with Martin at 3:00 PM today"* and *"Your next event is at 11:00 AM – A get together with your stockholders."*

When naming your tasks, you must take care to see you avoid the use of the first person. *"I'm home"* or *"I want the news"* will not be as Alexa-friendly as *"Arrive Home"* and *"News Update."*

How to Note events with precise time and people on your calendar

First, go with your mobile or computer browser and connect the Google channel. To improve on this functionality, use the **Slack Channel**(*ifttt.com/slack*) to connect this note with every member of your team or family. An alternate way to do this is to go to Amazon Alexa settings. Click on Calendar and pen in a new event.

How to Schedule for Repeated Tasks

Improve your schedule with the Google Calendar and your regular schedule. Do this daily or once every week to create more thinking space and organize your work schedule. For this, the **Trello channel**(*ifttt.com/trello*) will not only serve as a reminder for these repeating tasks but also help you make plans.

How To Share your workflow with the iOS phone

Create a workflow and connect the **Workflow Channel**(*ifttt.com/workflow*) and **Google Drive Channel**(*ifttt.com/google_drive*). This now enables you to share a webpage or text with Google Doc. If you use Slack, then you may send your message or web page. The two channels to connect are Slack Channel and Workflow Channel.

How To Order Uber

- Open the Alexa App and tap the three bar menu on Top Left Corner
- Tap Skills
- Under Skills, search for Uber
- Enable the Uber Skill
- Sign In to your Uber Account and tap Allow

For office-goers who use Uber often, pulling out the phone to call up Uber may become tedious. So, calling up Alexa seems to be more attractive. *"Alexa, Ask Uber for a ride."* And Alexa comes back with, *"Your Uber ride is on its way."* You understand the charm Echo has. One likes to talk to Alexa rather than a cab driver or manager anytime!

How To Set up DocSend Channel(*ifttt.com/docsend*)

Use this channel to keep track of the documents you send. Connect to various recipes and get informed when any person reads 100% of your document, post message to Slack channel whenever you have a new visit to a document, get an email of all the 100% document reads, remind me to follow up when someone reads 100% of my document (this could be your family member reading a family update) and much more. You can add this channel to these given here.

- **If Channel** (*ifttt.com/trackif*): You can use the Get Notifications from the If Channel if someone visits and reads 100% of your document.
- **FollowUp.cc** (*ifttt.com/ followupcc*): This helps our intrepid blogger or businessperson to keep 'with it'. You follow-up and see the reads. Connect first to start at this site.
- **Slack** (*ifttt.com/slack*): Post to the Slack Channel if you get a new visitor and if anyone reads 100% of your document.
- **ORBneXt** (*ifttt.com/ORBneXt*): In this, your Orb will flash when you have a visitor or anyone reads through the entire document.
- **Gmail**(*ifttt.com/gmail*): This is the most popular internet device and you can connect DocSend channel to improve communications. You will get an email when you have a visitor.

How To Setup a Square Channel(*ifttt.com/square*)

Square gives you the best way to allow payments by credit cards on your site. To activate this, you need to create a **Square account** (*bit.ly/amzeco*). You can use the connected services related to sales and payment.

- **Refunds**: When someone uses Square to make a new refund this adds a new line to your spreadsheet. Or better, you can receive an email to any account when you receive a refund over a specified amount.
- **Payments**: You get an email when money is credited to your Square account.
- **Funds heading into account**: Likewise, you can get a notification when funds are heading towards your account.

Square channel fits well with all the channels mentioned for the DocSend Channel such as ORBneXt and Gmail.

How to Integrate Blogging networks

Use one or many of the blog channels such as Blogger, WordPress, or Tumblr. You can add your business network when you use LinkedIn, Square, Slack, Quip or Salesforce.

- **Tumblr** (*ifttt.com/Tumblr*): With Tumblr, you can post your Instagram photos to your Tumblr blog. Further, you can publish selected Flickr images as Tumblr posts.
- **Blogger** (*ifttt.com/Blogger*): Here you can use many recipes to add content to your Blogger. For instance, Blog my Dropbox images and Share my new posts to Facebook provide an easy means to achieve your aim. Other people Push sweet Vimeo vids to my Blogger.
- **WordPress** (*ifttt.com/WordPress)*: WordPress is the favourite for many bloggers since it is stable and easy to use. Here with Echo, things have turned easier. The various recipes such as WP to Tumblr, Upload YouTube videos to WP blog, and Instagram to Blog help you publish your articles on the Internet with ease.

How to Speed up Complex Actions using Launch Center
(*ifttt.com/launch_center*)

Through this channel, you can add speed to your tasks. Launch Center Pro saves time by doing complex actions with a single command. You can use it to launch the Waze app when you leave home

- First get the Waze app.
- Set Launch Center Pro to get notifications.
- Now, you are ready to connect to the Launch Center Channel.

Chapter 4

STAY FIT WITH ECHO

Voice control is the doorway to future of technology. Smart watches and Smart TVs use smart surf. Echo takes this one step further with the voice controls for your exercise equipment. Try to begin with Fit Assist, Fitbit, Starfish Fit or Starfish Band and ALOP-Pilates-Class-Skill.

Keep up with health trends by getting updates from the New York Times. Add this and get regular emails on what clicks and what does not. For those who wish to keep track of their body measurements, use Withings app. Add the**Withings Channel**(*ifttt.com/withings*) and **Google Drive Channel**(*ifttt.com/google_drive*) first to begin. If you add the **Fitbit Channel** (*ifttt.com/fitbit*)you can save your Fitbit sleep logs to Google Drive. You can search these under recipes in IFTTT.

Connect with Fitbit

Use Fitbit to update your daily fitness goals. Though not as much interactive as you would like it to be, Fit Assist will tell you interesting facts on health and fitness upon request.

Amazon and Alexa do not store the data about your exercises but you use the interactions to update your goals daily. You will find this under skills in the alexa.amazon.com site.

How To Connect Fitbit through IFTTT

Go to this website and connect the two channels given there, the Fitbit channel and Google Calendar channel. Now, Alexa will remind you to go to sleep on time and adjust your sleep schedule according to the quality of sleep recorded the previous night. And you have your activity on a Google Spread sheet.

Alexa Skills for Exercise

For fitness freaks and exercise enthusiasts, there is a host of apps you can access.

Use the FitnessLogger

This Alexa skill helps you record your fitness schedule you follow. You can compare your workout you did the previous day and save the workout you did today. *"Alexa, ask FitnessLogger for all supported exercises"* will give you a list of workable exercises. Goto your Alexa app, to enable this skill.

7-Minute Workout

This skill helps you lower stress and cut fat. Enable this and use commands such as *"Alexa, start seven-minute workout"* or *"Alexa, start Workout."*

Training Tips

This set of tips helps the newcomers orient themselves to the gym workout. Enable this skill and use a command such as *"Alexa, ask Training Tips for tips today."*

Recon Channel(*ifttt.com/recon*)

Recon app is expensive but one of the trending eyewear technology to boost your connectivity. Meant for the Sports and Fitness category, you can get metrics projected to your eyepiece. This way you do not have to break your routine activity but you read the information. In this way, you can get news, calendar notifications, DubNation updates, sports news, and updates from your smartphone too. The unit costs $499 on Amazon. One may extend the capabilities of this app when you connect to third party apps with ANT+. Use the camera to get instant snaps of real events.

ALOP-Pilates-Class-Skill

This skill helps beginners to work out their Pilates exercises. *"Alexa, start Pilates class"* will take you through the exercise schedule. But first, you must enable this skill. Go to ALotOfPilates.com to get more details on the exercises.

Chapter 5

STREAM MUSIC ON YOUR ECHO

Alexa supports a growing number of free and subscription-based streaming services on Amazon devices

- Amazon Music
- Prime Music
- Spotify Premium
- Pandora
- TuneIn
- iHeartRadio
- Audible

Playback Commands

These commands will work with the following services

- Amazon Music
- Audible
- Prime Music

Say the **Alexa** word followed by any of the following commands.

- *"Alexa, Skip"*
- *"Alexa, Skip back"*
- *"Alexa, Pause"*
- *"Alexa, Continue"*

But some commands will vary with third party music streaming services like Spotify and TuneIn.

How to Migrate Your Music Files to Amazon

Your Amazon Echo device cannot playback any audio files that are stored in your Amazon Cloud Drive. However, the Echo can play files that are stored in your Amazon Music Library or Audible library, in case of audiobooks you own.

I am pleased to tell you that each Amazon customer has an account for Amazon Music Library. It does not matter whether you have signed up for premium version, you will have an account. If you look at the picture below, the link for you amazon drive is right there.

You can store up to 250 songs on your Music Library in Amazon for free. But, Amazon Prime members get unlimited access to the Amazon Prime Music Library. They are able to upload files from their Amazon Prime Music Library to their personal music libraries. The best part is that these files or the music you purchase online from Amazon does not count towards the 250-song free upload limit.

What if I have got a Large Playlist?

If you have got a huge, *personal* music library outside Amazon, it offers a premium subscription as well. For $24.99/year, you will be able to upload, play and store a max of 250,000 tracks. And the song purchases you make from Amazon do not count in this 250,000 track limit.

What if I don't want to migrate my Music to Amazon?

If you are like me and you don't want to go through the hassle of migrating your whole playlist to Amazon Music Player, I understand that totally....I have another solution for you. With Bluetooth, Alexa connects directly to either iTunes or Google

Music. You can pair Alexa to any device with Bluetooth using the following command:

- *"Alexa, Pair"*

Make sure your device is within the range for Echo. Once Alexa detects your device it will instruct you to go to it and select Echo from the Bluetooth pairing screen. Once the device is paired, open the app you normally use for iTunes / Google Music playback and start some music.

The commands you can use with Alexa for Bluetooth playback control:

- *"Alexa, Play"*
- *"Alexa, Pause"*
- *"Alexa, Restart"*
- *"Alexa, Resume"*
- *"Alexa, Stop"*
- *"Alexa, Previous"*
- *"Alexa, Next"*

How to Access Another Household Member's Music Library On Your Echo

To achieve this, set up *Amazon Household Profiles* in your Alexa app. This will give access of your Amazon account to the second person and also will allow that person to make purchases, both physical and digital, on your account using voice commands to the Echo.

You can prevent undesired purchases by adding a password. To setup the password,

- Go to the Voice Purchasing inside the Amazon Household Profile
- Enter a 4-digit confirmation code that users will speak at the time of purchases to confirm their identity.

After the Household Profile setup, you are able to switch accounts on you Echo and access all the content by using the following command

- *"Alexa, switch accounts"*

How to check whose profile is used currently

- *"Alexa, which account is this?"*

How to Buy Music using Echo

To shop for a song or an album use the following commands

- *"Alexa, Shop for the song [song name]"*
- *"Alexa, Shop for the album [album name]"*
- *"Alexa, Shop for the album [artist name]"*

Purchases are stored for free in your music library; they don't count against the storage limits, and are available for playback/download on any device that supports Amazon Music.

Connect with other Music Devices and Apps

Choose from the many devices to add quality to your music scene. iHeartRadio, TuneIn, Pandora and Spotify Premium top this list of must haves. And for those who have no subscriptions as yet to these channels, there always is the Amazon Music Library from where you can stream Prime Music.

How to Setup and Use Pandora on Echo?

- Tap on Alexa app
- Tap Menu in top left corner
- Open Music and Book and Tap Pandora in the sub menu.
- On the registration page for Pandora, tap *"Link account"*
- If you have a Pandora account Sign IN if not then Sign UP.

Once the setup process is completed, your station list will be seen on your Alexa app.

iHeartRadio

This radio station has a wide range of genres ranging from Hip Hop and R&B, Top 40 & Pop, Classic Rock, Oldies, Jazz and much more.

TuneIn

TuneIn likewise has many genres though the crowd here is younger. You can also use Tunein to listen to your favourite Podcasts.

- *"Alexa, Play [number on the dial] [station name] on TuneIn"*
- *"Alexa, play [podcast name] on TuneIn"*

Alexa Skills for Music

This section has plenty of apps and one only needs the time to go through it. Here we list some important ones that would be of interest. Add the stations to Echo and you have a good selection of songs to listen to all the time.

Fluffy Radio

A favourite with radio music listeners, Fluffy Radio helps you make requests and stream the songs through TuneIn. *"Alexa, ask Fluffy Radio to request Silent Night."* Or, *"Alexa, open Fluffy Radio."* This is a fun way to listen to songs.

Spotify Premium

You have to sign up and buy one of their music packs. This monthly pack starts at $19 and goes on to $29, $59.99 and $79.99.

Tune your Guitar

This is an amazingly handy Skill. Just follow these steps and your will have a tuned guitar.

- In the Alexa Skills menu, search for Guitar Tuner.

- Use the following command, "Alexa, ask Guitar Tuner to tune my guitar."
- The tuning will start in the following tone sequence: from low E to high E and everything in-between.
- Tune until you have and tuned Guitar.

IFTTT Integration for Music

Gone are the touch and gestures to control your smartphone, your room air-conditioner, and those lights. Say it and Echo will do it. Gone too are the days when all you could do is wish that the boring music would stop. Now you can and switch to a channel that has your kind of music playing.

Music is only as good as its clarity. Listen to a bunch of vague sounds without a beat or harmony and you will get a headache. This is why music lovers attempt to ensure their selection has the right sound and the right mood.

Set up the smart Hi-Fi system in every room. Connect to**Musaic**(*ifttt.com/musaic*) to improve the sound quality of your music. If you connect the lights to Music, you will get party lights when the music begins. Also, you can wake up with music streaming and night-lights fade.

And don't miss out on the **Deezer channel** (*ifttt.com/deezer*). With Deezer, you can take your music with you to every place you go. Use Add new tracks to make a fast addition of the tracks you want to Deezer.

- Sync your favourite songs to **SoundCloud** (*ifttt.com/soundcloud*)
- Add artist
- List favourite songs on **Evernote** (*ifttt.com/evernote*)
- Listen to favourites from SoundCloud on Deezer
- Add favorite to Google spreadsheet

Connect to music with Musixmatch (*ifttt.com/musixmatch*)

Connect your favorite songs to Musixmatch.

Spotify Playlist

For those who have an Apple account, you can create a Spotify playlist from your Apple Music Playlist. Connect to **Spotify Channel** (*ifttt.com/spotify*) and **Workflow Channel** (*ifttt.com/ workflow*) to begin.

SoundCloud

This app SoundCloud has many recipes that give music a new meaning. Share your SoundCloud tracks to Facebook; sync them to your Spotify collection; Use **Genius** (*ifttt.com/genius*) to follow the songs you like on SoundCloud or share new songs to Tumblr.

Chapter 6

SAFETY

Is Alexa Spying On You?

No. Alexa is not spying on you. Alexa only pays attention to you when it hears the designated wake word. Rest of the time, although technically it is on all the time and always on a look out for the wake word from you, it does not record your voice.

But if you are still worried that Alexa will hear and record any private conversations, you can push MUTE. Do remember to hold it until the LED ring turns red. Now Alexa will not hear anything neither will it respond until you switch off the mute button.

There have been zero cases of people using Echo for illegal activities till date. However, to take further precaution and prevent any kind of monkey business from your Echo device ensure that you:

- Do not position the Amazon Echo near any window.
- Do not position the Echo close to any speakerphone or answering machine.
- Mute your Amazon Echo device when away from home.

Amazon's official response to privacy concerns as follows:

"Echo only streams recordings from the user's home when the 'wake word' activates the device, though the device is technically capable of streaming voice recordings at all times, and in fact will always be listening to detect if a user has uttered the word."[1]

However you need to know that Echo uses machine learning to study your voice pattern from past recordings and improve its response to your questions. You can delete these voice recordings, but in doing so you may degrade your user experience with Echo.

How to delete your Voice Recordings

Delete Individual Recordings

- Open your Amazon Echo app
- Tap Settings
- Tap History.
- Here, you will see a list of requests you have made since setting up your Echo.
- To delete a recording, tap it, then tap Delete voice recordings.

Delete All the Recordings

- Head to **Amazon** (*amazon.com/myx*)
- Sign in and click Your Devices.
- Select Amazon Echo,
- Click *Manage Voice Recordings*

Troubleshooting

Sometimes the Echo does not listen to your voice or hangs carry out the following steps to get it back in action.

- Ensure that your device in not on MUTE. Check the LED ring in not RED. If it is RED, press the MUTE button again and start speaking.
- Ensure that Echo is not receiving a software update.
- Unplug the device and leave it off for 60 sec and then plug it back again. It should mostly come back online by performing this action.
- If it still does not respond, leave it unplugged for a few hours and then plug it back again.
- Still Struggling? Try to your Echo. You will need to setup the device again so try to use this step sparingly. However, in most cases this does the trick.
- If the problem still persists, try to contact Amazon Customer Support.

Chapter 7

EASTER EGGS AND TIPS

Though the future is far away, there is no reason for us to not use the future technology today. Echo may need to cover many more milestones to achieve perfection but the state it made is good enough. After all, one can search and find Easter eggs that the bunny (Echo) has hidden away.

Fun Phrases to Try Out with Alexa

Here is a list of fun phrases you can try out with Echo. This list has been compiled from various sources on the net and is not an exhaustive list as Echo development team keeps on publishing more phrases regularly.

- What is your favourite colour?
- Do you have a boyfriend?
- Where do babies come from?
- Which comes first; chicken or egg?
- Do aliens exist?
- Where do you live?
- Do you want to build a snowman?
- What is love?
- Who won best actor Oscar in 1973?
- May the force be with you!
- Who let the dogs out?
- To be or not to be?
- Who loves ya baby?
- Who is the walrus?
- How tall are you?
- Where are you from?
- Do you want to fight?
- Do you want to play a game?

- I think you are funny?
- Is the cake a lie?

- Random fact
- Roll a dice
- Tell me a joke
- Mac or PC?
- Give me a hug
- Are you lying?
- How many angels can dance?
- I want the truth
- What's in the name?
- Knock knock
- What are you wearing?
- Rock paper scissors
- Party time
- Make me breakfast
- Where are my keys?
- Do you know the way to San Jose?
- Party on, Wayne
- Beam me up
- Make me sandwich
- How much does the earth weigh?
- Tea. Earl Grey. Hot.
- Who is your daddy?

- Is there Santa?
- Best Tablet

- When is the end of the world?
- How many roads must a man walk down?
- Count by Ten
- Can you give me some Money? (Ask twice)
- Do you believe in ghosts?
- Do you believe in god?
- Do you believe in life after love?
- Do you know Siri?
- Do you like green eggs and ham?
- Do you really want to hurt me?
- Fire photon torpedoes
- Good night
- High five!
- How do i get rid of a dead body?
- Do you make bread?
- How many calories are in (name a food)?
- Live long and prosper
- Never gonna give you up
- One fish, two fish
- I'm home
- I've fallen and I can't get up
- I am your father
- I have seen things you people wouldn't believe.
- Tell me a story
- Will you marry me?

Special Animal Sounds

Meantime, you can have loads of fun with special music and soundtracks. Amazon Prime members have access to this while non-members have to pay $0.89 for each track of animal sounds. The tracks themselves are interesting and you should look at the customer reviews of each one before you purchase them. You can get the best ones that way with ease. The collections include bird sounds (favorite with nature lovers and meditation freaks), animal sounds ("Alexa, what did the dog say this morning") and various mixes.

Maker Channel*(ifttt.com/maker)*

If you want to get involved in this product, you can do it via the Maker Channel. You may connect your DIY project to this channel to share your experience with others. Go to *huckster.io* to share your experience with others.

Conclusion

Hope this book has helped you make Amazon Echo the centre of your smart life and enabled you to organise your life seamlessly with Alexa at your command.

Continue on with your wonderful discovery of the power of Echo and Tap. Hope your doubts are removed and your life has eased. Since this is only the beginning, you will find more comfort and happiness from Alexa as you get more fluent with the device and the interface.

This is just the beginning, the Alexa rage is going to go global very soon and then you will see an explosion of Alexa Skills that will transform the way we live.

Wish you all the best automation possible in your life! Ah, Alexa! Come sit down.

Hope you liked this book...Or did you

Your Opinion is Valuable to us. Please leave a review for this book.

And if want to learn some real DIY hack on your new Amazon Echo do get in touch at kindletechgames@gmail.com

References

Further Resources

Amazon Echo Wikipedia - *bit.ly/amzecowiki*

Amazon Alexa Skill Central - *alexaskillscentral.com*

IFTTT-*ifttt.com*

Love my echo -*lovemyecho.com*

Echo Tricks -*echotricks.com*

Echosim - *echosim.io*

Alexa - *alexa.amazon.com*

IFTTT Recipes

Evernote- *bit.ly/amzeco1*

Gmail - *bit.ly/amzeco2*

Todoist - *bit.ly/amzeco3*

ios Reminders - *bit.ly/amzeco4*

Google Calendar -*bit.ly/amzeco100*

IFTTT Channels

ifttt.com/danalock

ifttt.com/dlink_smart_plug

ifttt.com/ge_appliances_refrigerator

ifttt.com/weather

ifttt.com/netatmo_welcome

ifttt.com/signul_beacon

ifttt.com/relay

ifttt.com/wemo_switch

ifttt.com/hue

ifttt.com/workflow

ifttt.com/slack

ifttt.com/trello

ifttt.com/workflow

ifttt.com/google_drive

ifttt.com/docsend

ifttt.com/trackif

ifttt.com/followupcc

ifttt.com/slack

ifttt.com/ORBneXt

ifttt.com/Gmail

ifttt.com/square

ifttt.com/Tumblr

ifttt.com/Blogger

ifttt.com/WordPress

ifttt.com/launch_center

ifttt.com/withings

ifttt.com/google_drive

ifttt.com/fitbit

ifttt.com/recon

ifttt.com/musaic

ifttt.com/deezer

ifttt.com/soundcloud

ifttt.com/evernote

ifttt.com/musixmatch

ifttt.com/musixmatch

ifttt.com/spotify

ifttt.com/workflow

ifttt.com/genius

ifttt.com/maker

*Y*ou May Also Like

Amazon Echo Dot
Advanced User Guide

Get your Copy Now!

www.amazon.com/dp/B01MQFDHGF/

Made in the USA
Charleston, SC
24 February 2017